CW01548129

Samhain in Your Pocket

A Tiny Little Book About the
Celtic Origins of Halloween

♣

I. E. KNEVERDAY

ISBN: 9798351121147

For things that go bump in the night

6 HALLOWEEN CUSTOMS THAT ORIGINATED WITH THE ANCIENT CELTS

1) Bobbing for Apples
Why do we bob for apples on Halloween?

Halloween - Bobbing for Apples, 1908
by Salem State Archives

Nothing says "Halloween fun" quite like plunging your face into a bucket of water in the hopes of getting an apple wedged between your teeth like you're some kind of prized pig preparing yourself for a roast. I mean, seriously… where the hell did this bizarre, semi-aquatic autumnal custom come from?

Go back a couple of centuries, and you might have witnessed courtly lords and ladies bobbing for apples in an effort to foretell their romantic futures. In Britain, a common version of the game was to have each floating apple correspond to a potential mate. Young women would take turns aiming their chompers at the apples named for the young men they fancied. Get the apple on the first try, and the relationship was bound to blossom. Get it on the second try, and sparks would fly at first but then the relationship would fizzle. Get it on the third try, and the poor young lady might as well spit it out — the relationship just wasn't meant to be.

In Ireland, apple bobbing is more commonly known as "snap apple." This variation of the game typically sees players lunging teeth-first at apples the ingredients were there for a tradition like apple bobbing to develop.

It should also be mentioned that apples have a special place in Irish mythology. For example, the sea-god Manannán Mac Lir is said to rule a paradisiacal island called Emain Ablach ("Emain of the apple trees'), where apple trees bear fruit and blossoms simultaneously. What's more, the voyage of the famed Irish hero Bran begins with a mysterious woman giving him a silver branch with a white blossom from one of Emain Ablach's trees.

The story of Emain Ablach would go on to influence another apple-filled island paradise: Avalon, from Arthurian legend. In Welsh, Avalon is called Ynys Afallach ("lsle of Afallach"). The Welsh word for apple is *afall*.

But enough about apples. Everyone knows the *real* symbol of Halloween is the pumpkin… right?

2. Carving Pumpkins
Why do we carve pumpkins on Halloween?

Photo by Kelly Sikkema on Unsplash

I will explore this topic in-depth in my chapter on the history of the jack-o'-lantern, so here's the abridged version:

Long before anyone was carving pumpkins on Halloween, the ancient Irish were carving faces into turnips, beets, and potatoes on Samhain and sticking coals or candles inside of them to create lanterns.

According to Irish folklore, this was done to commemorate the suffering of Stingy Jack, a blacksmith who tricked the devil and, as a result, was cursed to wander the bogs for all eternity with only a carved turnip lantern to light his way.

That's the origin of the name jack-o'-lantern (Jack of the Lantern), and it was originally used to describe the phenomenon of *ignis fatuus* (a.k.a "will-o'-the-wisps" a.k.a." fairy lights" a.k.a. "fool's fire"), wherein gases released by decomposing organic matter combust above peat bogs.

But enough about flaming bog farts. Here's how jack-o'-lanterns became associated with Halloween:

On Samhain, fires were supposed to be extinguished and rekindled from ceremonial fires lit by druids. To facilitate the transfer of this fire, coals were placed into lanterns made from root vegetables. (Remember: Samhain marked the end of the harvest season, so there were plenty of root vegetables to go around.) As Nathan Mannion, senior curator of Dublin's Irish Emigration Museum, explains:

"Metal lanterns were quite expensive, so people would hollow out root vegetables. Over time people started to carve faces and designs to allow light to shine through the holes without extinguishing the ember," (source: *National Geographic*).

The carved faces also served another purpose: to scare away any vengeful spirits, demons, fairies, etc. that happened to cross over from the Celtic Otherworld during Samhain, as the evening of October 31st was believed to be a time when the barriers between the land of the living and the land of the dead became permeable.

Flash forward to the 19th century, and millions of Irish immigrants bring their tradition of carving root vegetables on Halloween with them to North America. Only, when they get here, they discover a rotund native vegetable that is much better suited to the art form: the pumpkin. The rest, as they say, is Halloween history.

3. Decorating With Black and Orange
Why are black and orange the colors of Halloween

Photo by Bee Felten-Leidel on Unsplash

At first glance, this one seems self-explanatory: black is scary and orange is the color of pumpkins. So, naturally, they became Halloween's go-to color combo. Put a black and orange bow on it, this mystery has been solved. Except…that's not it. That's not it at all.

In order to understand why black and orange became the colors of Halloween, we once again need to look back to Halloween's Celtic progenitor, Samhain. Let's tackle black first.

Turns out, black wasn't associated with Samhain because it's the color of spookiness, but because it's the color of death and mourning. And what is Samhain if not a celebration of death?

The festival is centered around the dead who have passed on to the Celtic Otherworld (but who might make an appearance on the evening of October 31st) as well as the figurative death of the sun as winter approaches. To quote Whiskey Stevens, author of *Rise of the Witch*: "Black is a representation of the dark months that come with winter," (source: "What Are the Halloween Colors and What Do They Mean?, *Reader's Digest*).

So, what about orange? It's gotta be the pumpkins right? Making jack-o'-lanterns, after all, has been a Samhain tradition for centuries. But remember: in the last section, we learned that Celtic peoples originally used root vegetables for making jack-o'-lanterns. Pumpkin-carving came later. And by then, orange had already been well-established as a color of Halloween. What gives?

Here's a clue: go rub two sticks together. Bonus points if those sticks have a few fall leaves attached to them.

Allow me to be less cryptic: it's likely that orange represents the ceremonial Samhain fires lit by druids on the evening of October 31st. As I mentioned earlier, the coals from those community fires would be transported via jack-o'-lantern and used to reignite the hearths in people's homes that had been left to burn out.

Of course, there's also the prevalence of the color orange in autumn leaves, which may have reinforced the idea of orange being a Samhain color. As Stevens explains:

"Orange is representative of the fire that burns during the festival of Samhain and during the winter months. It also corresponds to the leaves that have changed color and of the harvest itself."

4. Dressing Up in Costumes
Why do we wear costumes on Halloween?

Photo by Clay LeConey on Unsplash

Some of you may find this hard to believe, but there was a time, many moons ago, when children dressed up on Halloween not as superheroes or princesses, but as ghosts and goblins and all manner of ghoulish, ghastly, terrifying creatures.

Shocking, I know. But this is pretty much how the Samhain tradition of wearing costumes originated: the goal wasn't to appear cute or strong or extravagant, it was to disguise oneself from—or potentially blend in with—the supernatural beings crossing over from the Otherworld. That meant adopting a frightening appearance.

Starting in the 16th century, if not earlier, groups known as "mummers" or "guisers" would pay homage to this Celtic custom by galavanting around in costumes on Halloween.

Here's how author and folklorist Florence Marian McNeill explained guising and its origin in her 1961 book, *The Silver Bough Volume Three: A Calendar of Scottish National Festivals – Hallowe'en to Yule* (note: This same passage also appears in her 1970 work, *Hallowe'en: Its Origin, Rites and Ceremonies in the Scottish Tradition*):

"[T]here is nothing even nominally Christian about the Hallowe'en guisers. It is thought that they may have originated in a folk-memory of the actual initiators at the Druidic feast, who, as masked men, represented spirits, but until fairly recent times their object was to avoid being recognised by the spirits of their dead, who might possibly do them a mischief.

"To-day, the grotesque masks and fantastic garments of the guisers represent the uncanny creatures whom their forefathers believed to be at large on this occult night—ghoulies, ghaisties and bogies; fairies, banshees and gruagachs; witches, warlocks and wurricoes; brownies, urisks and shelly-coats; kelpies and water-bulls; spunkies, gnomes, trolls and sprites: the whole unhallowed clanjamfrey of the netherworld."

Let's pause for a moment to appreciate McNeill's use of the word "clanjamfrey," which is officially my new favorite word of all time.

It might also be interesting to learn that in addition to the wearing of "grotesque masks and fantastic garments" on Halloween, face-painting appears to have its origin in Samhain as well—and it's directly connected to those ceremonial bonfires we've heard so much about in previous sections. To quote McNeill:

"Instead of masks, some of the guisers have blackened faces. This is a relic of the blackening with the ashes of the Druidical bonfire for protection and good fortune."

5. Giving Out Candy

Why do we give out candy on Halloween?

Photo by Branden Skeli on Unsplash

As we learned earlier from journalist Alison Richards, ancient Celts "tied apples to evergreen branches" on

Samhain to encourage the return of their sun deity. Richards goes on to tell us that in that same vein, "[g]ifts of fruit and nuts, and animal sacrifices, were offered to the gods."

Anthropologist Walter Evans-Wentz bolsters this claim in his book, *The Fairy-Faith in Celtic Countries* (1911), noting:

"Samain... was the great Celtic feast of the dead when offerings or sacrifice of various kinds were made to ancestral spirits, and to the Tuatha De Danann and the spirit-hosts under their control."

For those unfamiliar with the Tuatha De Danann (also spelled "De Danaan"), they are the old gods of Irish mythology, known for "their supremacy over ghosts and demons on Samain and their power to steal mortals away at such a time."

Needless to say, it was important to make offerings to these guys (and gals), lest they unleash a fire-breathing, timpán-playing monster from the Otherworld, which is exactly what happens in the story of Aillén. To quote Evans-Wentz:

"Aillén visits Tara, the old psychic centre both for Ireland's high-kings and its Druids. He comes as it were against the conquerors of his race, who in their neglectfulness no longer render due worship and sacrifice on the Feast of Samain to the Tuatha De Danann, the gods of the dead, at that time supreme; and then it is that he works his magic against the royal palaces of the kings and Druids on the ancient Hill."

After being conquered by the invading Milesians and driven underground (or so the story goes), the Tuatha de Danann grew smaller in popular imaginations—both literally and figuratively. The powerful gods of old became the *aes sídhe*—"the people of the hills"—otherwise known as fairies. But their connection to Samhain, and their perceived potential for mischief-making, remained strong. Thus, later generations of Celtic peoples began leaving sweet treats out on their doorsteps on the evening of October 31st to appease the fairies and whatever demons and restless spirits might be in their company.

Even after Samhain was (nominally) Christianized, people continued this tradition, albeit with a more personal twist. It became less about appeasing sinister fairies and spirits and more about accommodating the homesick souls of loved ones who'd passed on. As the aforementioned author and folklorist Florence Marian McNeill explains:

"All over Europe, the souls of the departed were believed to revisit their old homes on the eve of Allhallows and warm themselves at the fire or regale themselves with the food and drink set out for them by their kinsfolk."

Eventually, people began leaving out a specific type of sweet treat for the souls that visited on All Hallows Eve: soul cakes. Made with raisins, cinnamon, ginger, and nutmeg, the soul cake was the forerunner to Halloween candy.

6. Trick-or-Treating
Why do we go trick-or-treating on Halloween?

Photo by Haley Phelps on Unsplash

So, to recap the previous two sections: we've got people going about in costume on All Hallows Eve to disguise themselves from spirits, and we've got people leaving sweet treats out on their front stoops on that same night to appease those same spirits. Clearly, the conditions were perfect for a new All Hallows Eve tradition to develop:

Burning witches.

No, wait…trick-or-treating.

I meant trick-or-treating.

This tradition likely got its start when villagers and townsfolk dressed as ghosts and fairies and demons and the like began accepting (re: stealing) Samhain offerings on behalf of those otherworldly beings they were impersonating. Upon arriving at homes that didn't have any treats on offer, the disguised Samhain revelers perpetrated acts of mischief in recompense.

As a result, people eventually began giving out sweet treats on the evening of October 31st to appease not the spirits, but their costumed impersonators. This is the foundation upon which modern trick-or-treating is built. To quote husband and wife authors Vince and Sandra Peddle, who write under the pen name S. V. Peddle:

"Today's popular Halloween custom of 'trick or treat', although believed to be an American import, can be traced to these ancient European customs of appeasing the dead. The children who call on households on Halloween night with the choice between good and bad luck (trick or treat, give me a sweet or I'll do something nasty to you), personify the old spirits of the winter, who demanded reward in exchange for good fortune." (source: *Pagan Channel Islands: Europe's Hidden Heritage,* 2007).

Of course, there would be several steps in the development of trick-or-treating: it didn't jump directly from rabble-rousers impersonating spirits to children roaming neighborhoods collecting candy.

In one of its medieval iterations, known as "souling," poor people would go to wealthy homes on All Hallows Eve and say prayers for the souls of deceased loved ones and/or give performances in exchange for money and food. By the 19th century, it was common for households to give out nuts and fruits (apples in particular) to costumed children on Halloween. And by the 1920s, candy had entered the mix; the age of modern trick-or-treating—and some might say the age of modern Halloween —had arrived.

*'The Christian practice of souling on All Hallows' Eve,
also known as Halloween, in an English town. The
photograph is taken from* St. Nicholas: An Illustrated
Magazine for Young Folks, *December 1882, p. 93.
The magazine states that the rich gave soul cakes to the poor
on Halloween; in return the recipients prayed for
the souls of the givers and their friends." (source:
Wikimedia Commons)*

1. HOW DO YOU PRONOUNCE SAMHAIN?

First things first:
If you've been pronouncing it "Sam-hane" this whole time, you've been doing it wrong.

Samhain, the ancient Celtic end-of-summer/beginning-of-winter festival, from which our modern holiday of Halloween was spawned, originated with the Goidelic-/Gaelic-speaking Celts of Ireland.

One of four cross-quarter day feasts —the others being Imbolc, Beltane, and Lughnasa—Samhain was of such importance to the Irish Gaels, the word itself became ingrained in their language.

As Irish pagan author Lora O'Brien notes, Samhain is "a word that has a huge cultural and historical foundation as well as a place in modern spoken Irish language as the calendar word for the month of November."

According to O'Brien, deliberately mispronouncing the word Samhain, when you know the correct pronunciation of Samhain is just a Google search (or, at this point, just a few sentences) away, is disrespectful to Irish culture.

"You don't get to just take someone else's heritage and language and change the pronunciation because it's 'how you've always said it'. Don't do that.

"Out of all the Pagan festivals, this one is most specifically rooted in Irish traditions, and is perhaps the most bastardised by modern culture around 'Halloween'…"

So for all of my readers who are not Irish-speakers, myself included, let's show some respect this Samhain holiday season, shall we?

THE PROPER WAY(S) TO PRONOUNCE SAMHAIN

I will defer to O'Brien on this one: The correct way to pronounce Samhain is "Sow-wen, with sow as in female pig."

To clarify, that is the proper pronunciation of Samhain in Irish (*Gaeilge*).

The website PronounceItRight.com concurs with the "sow-as-in-female-pig" approach to Samhain pronunciation.

And I quote: "Samhain is usually pronounced in its Irish version. So the correct pronunciation of Samhain in Irish is Sau-ihn. The first part, -Sau, is pronounced like the "sow", the female of a pig."

The website opts for a slightly different phonetic spelling of Samhain, "Sau-ihn" versus O'Brien's "Sow-wen", but the end result is nearly the same.

And while they may not yield you a perfect pronunciation of the word Samhain, if such a thing even exists, both Samhain pronunciations—"Sau-ihn" and "Sow-wen"—get you much closer to the authentic item than the oft-spoken (but incorrect) "Sam-hane".

BREAKING DOWN
THE PRONUNCIATION
OF SAMHAIN
SYLLABLE BY SYLLABLE

For those who wish to go above and beyond the call of duty—the duty, in this case, being the need to pronounce a word in a way that respects the language and culture it comes from—the aforementioned pronunciation website offers a syllable-by-syllable breakdown of how one should go about pronouncing Samhain.

The first syllable of Samhain we already covered: "Sow," like a female pig.

The second syllable of Samhain is "pronounced somewhat midway between an 'i' and an 'e' sound." This explains the discrepancy between the website's phonetic spelling of Samhain (Sau-**i**hn) and O'Brien's (Sow-w**e**n): the English alphabet can't provide the precise sound that is needed, so choices have to be made.

The Irish film critic Brian Lloyd, for example, chose differently: He maintains that Sow-unn is the proper pronunciation.

"Samhain. You pronounce it Sow-Unn. Say it again – Sow-Unn," he wrote in an article for Entertainment.ie. The article was in response to the Netflix series *The Chilling Adventures of Sabrina*'s constant mispronunciation of Samhain.

As Lloyd noted, "Irish people and pagans who know how to pronounce Samhain have been enjoying how the series regularly butchers the word."

Now, onto the third syllable of Samhain.

Yes, you heard me correctly.

In another variation of the phonetic spelling of Samhain, one that attempts to make up for the lack of the English alphabet's dexterity, one adds a Spanish "ñ" to the end of the word. Thus, Sau-ihn becomes Sau-ih**ñ**.

To quote PronounceItRight.com: "Adding that sound, the pronunciation of Samhain becomes Sau-ihn(ye), where the -ye is basically just the initial pronunciation of the 'y'. It resembles a shorter 'ñ' sound like the word 'piñata'. So if you pronounce the 'n' in -ihn as an 'ñ', but stopping midway through it you achieve the proper pronunciation of Samhain in Irish, which would equate to Sau-ihñ."

REGIONAL VARIATIONS IN SAMHAIN PRONUNCIATION

So far we've focused on the Irish pronunciation of Samhain, but it turns out the first results Google spits out when you search for "how to pronounce Samhain" are the British and American pronunciations:

"Sown" for British English, and "Saa · wn" for American English.

Weird that Google Search displays these two phonetic spellings in its little header widget thingy but not an Irish one.

But I digress...

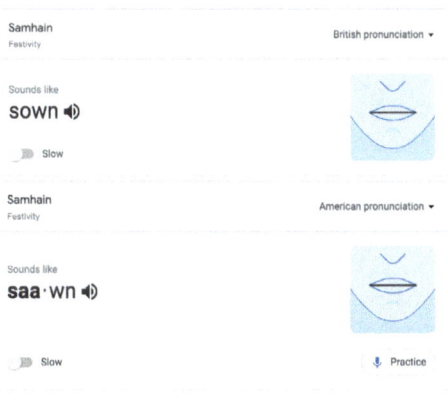

source: Google

Regional variations in the pronunciation of Samhain also occur within Ireland. The on-line Dictionary and Language Library, developed by Foras na Gaeilge in parallel with the New English-Irish Dictionary project, provides three distinct pronunciations of Samhain. (They're audio clips, FYI, so the phonetic spellings are my best attempts at interpreting what I heard.)

ULSTER DIALECT
🔊 listen...

CONNACHT DIALECT
🔊 listen...

MUNSTER DIALECT
🔊 listen...

source: teanglann.ie/en/fuaim/Samhain
^Go listen for yourself!

- Ulster: **Sah-win**

- Connacht: **Soun**
  (like "sound" without the "d")

- Munster: **Sow-in**

THE SCOTTISH GAELIC PRONUNCIATION OF SAMHAIN (SAMHUINN)

Finally, the Scots have "their own pronunciation stuff going on," to quote O'Brien. She's alluding to the fact that the Scottish word for Samhain, Samhuinn, is pronounced with a slight "v" sound at the start of the second syllable.

So in Scottish Gaelic, Samhain is pronounced Sah-vin.

This according to a Scottish Gaelic speaker, who went on to note that the "mh" in Samhuinn is pronounced "somewhere between a 'v' and a 'w'" whereas "it's pretty much completely a 'w' in Irish…sow-en."

2. WHAT IS SAMHAIN?
DEFINITION &
ETYMOLOGY

Is it just me, or has there been a huge push in recent years around what I'm calling, for lack of a better phrase, "Samhain awareness"?

Yes, the rise of Irish mythology in popular culture is one factor, of which Samhain is no doubt a beneficiary. But more than that, I think it's safe to say there's been a push, especially in the past few years, toward properly recognizing and crediting and celebrating the cultural origins of the art and music—and festivals —many of us know and love today.

Granted, not everybody's gonna get it right. (You know the saying: the road to Tech Duinn is paved with good intentions.)

For example, as mentioned in the previous chapter, in 2018 there was an uproar—at least among Irish, Scottish, and neopagan online communities— around the repeated mispronunciation of "Samhain" on the Netflix series *The Chilling Adventures of Sabrina.*

Now, if you've been a long-time reader of IrishMyths.com (and/or a student of mythological studies, druidism, paganism, Wicca, etc.), there's a strong chance you already have a sufficient understanding of what Samhain is all about.

But for the sake of thoroughness, and for the sake of my own edification, I've challenged myself to define Samhain, placing a premium on conciseness.

SAMHAIN, DEFINED:

Samhain (also: Samain) was a pastoral/ harvest festival celebrated—under various names—across the Celtic world on the evening of October 31st and into November 1st with ceremonial fires and other rituals. An important—if not the most important—holiday on the Celtic calendar, Samhain marks the midway point between the autumnal equinox and the winter solstice, making it one of four Celtic cross-quarter days. (The other three, as a reminder, are Imbolc, Beltane, and Lughnasa).

As noted by historian Peter Berresford Ellis, the "Feis na Samhain," or the festival of Samhain, was also a Celtic New Year celebration, marking "the end of one pastoral year and the commencement of the next," (source: *A Dictionary of Irish Mythology*, 1987). Ellis also describes Samhain as "an intensely spiritual time for it was the period when the Otherworld became visible to mankind and when spiritual forces were let loose on the human world."

Professor and folklorist Juilene Osborne-McKnight expands on this notion of the Otherworld becoming visible in her definition of Samhain, noting that on Samhain, "the veil that separated this world from the world of the Others (An Sidhe) grew thin," (source: *The Story We Carry in our Bones: Irish History for Americans*).

This thinning of the membrane between worlds meant that ghosts and fairies and all manner of otherworldly creatures could cross over on Samhain and wreak havoc.

To quote Osborne-McKnight:

"On this night, of all nights, our ancestors believed that the souls of the dead could return and the Little People could come through the doorway. The Little People could be…unpredictable. Among their number were those who cared for human beings, married them, dealt fairly with them. But there were equally as many who might try to kill humans, steal their children and replace them with changeling babies, or trick them into the world of the Sidhe, in which time did not pass the same way it passes on earth. A human tricked into the world of the Sidhe might believe that he had been among them for three days, only to return to earth to discover that 300 years had passed and everyone he knew was long dead."

Yeah…not ideal. So what did the ancient Irish do on Samhain to protect against such supernatural shenanigans? Welp, as I explained in the introduction, they basically came up with shenanigans of their own.

Riders of the Sidhe *(1911), painting by John Duncan*

Or as Osborne-McKnight puts it: "Samhain was a dangerous time in the Celtic mind and numerous rituals evolved as protection. Our ancestors might have left out food and drink as a gift for the Others or worn masks to frighten them away. Skulls with candles in them might have been hung in trees either to invite these spirits of the dead or to scare off the Sidhe."

It's easy to see how such rituals would lay the groundwork for the modern holiday of Halloween. Granted, there was one stepping stone in-between:

Christianization.

As Ellis notes: "Christianity took this pagan festival over as a harvest festival. The feast became St. Martin's Mass (Martinmas). The festival also became All Saints' Day or All-Hallows and the evening prior was Hallowe'en, still celebrated as the night when spirits and ghosts set out to wreak vengeance on the living and when evil marches unbridled across the world."

Ellis goes on to describe the ceremonial Samhain fires lit by the ancient druids, from which all hearth fires had to be lit.

In Ireland, as in the other Celtic countries, the fires were extinguished and could only be rekindled from a ceremonial fire lit by the druids at Samhain on Tlachtga (now the Hill of Ward).

FYI: Samhain bonfires continue to be staples of modern Samhain celebrations, i.e. those conducted by neopagans, neo-druids, Wiccans, and the like.

The custom of Samhain fires is also closely linked to the modern Halloween tradition of carving jack-o'-lanterns. Indeed, it's likely the ancient Irish transported embers from the Samhain fires to their own hearths in hollowed-out turnips. (Pumpkins, being native to the Americas, would not be used for making jack-o'-lanterns until the 19th century).

"Jack-O-Lantern" by photographer IrishFireside, Flickr.
The jack-o'-lantern pictured dates from 1903 and was carved at Baile na Finne, Co.
Donegal. It now resides at the Irish Museum of Country Life.
(source:@irarchaeology)

THE ETYMOLOGY OF
SAMHAIN

According to author and librarian Ruth Edna Kelley, the reason Samhain and, by extension, Halloween, are so closely associated with death and evil and fire has everything to do with the changing of the seasons and, specifically, the "suffering" of the sun.

"On November first was Samhain ("summer's end")…The year was over, and the sun's life of a year was done. The Celts thought that at this time the sun fell a victim for six months to the powers of winter darkness…

"From the idea that the sun suffered from his enemies on this day grew the association of Samhain with death," (source: *The Book of Hallowe'en,* 1919).

Kelley also reveals to us in the above quotation the meaning of the word Samhain—or at least a popular interpretation of it: "summer's end."

Author Clement A. Miles reiterates the "summer's end" etymology of Samhain, while also offering an alternative:

"The Celtic year…appears to have begun in November with the feast of Samhain—a name that may mean either 'summer-end' or 'assembly'," (source: *Christmas In Ritual and Tradition, Christian and Pagan,* 1912).

If accurate, the "assembly" interpretation may hearken back to Samhain's origins as a harvest festival.

Rather than being a morbid affair, perhaps those first Samhains were about people coming together and sharing their recently harvested crops, feasting and festing not only in celebration of the dead, but in celebration of the persistence of life.

To quote Scottish scholar and folklore researcher J.A. MacCulloch:

"The great commemoration of the dead was held on Samhain eve, a festival intended to aid the dying powers of vegetation, whose life, however, was still manifested in evergreen shrubs, in the mistletoe, in the sheaf of corn from last harvest—the abode of the corn-spirit...

"[On] Samhain, beginning the Celtic year...The powers of blight were beginning their ascendancy, yet the future triumph of the powers of growth was not forgotten. Probably Samhain had gathered up into itself other feasts occurring earlier or later. Thus it bears traces of being a harvest festival, the ritual of the earlier harvest feast [Lugnasad] being transferred to the winter feast, as the Celts found themselves in lands where harvest is not gathered before late autumn…

"Samhain may thus be regarded as, in origin, an old pastoral and agricultural festival, which in time came to be looked upon as affording assistance to the powers of growth in their conflict with the powers of blight," (source: *The Religion of the Ancient Celts*, 1911).

There is one final etymological interpretation of "Samhain" that bears mentioning, courtesy of PronounceItRight.com (which, yes, was a resource I used for the previous chapter).

The website makes clear that the "origin of the word Samhain is not entirely known," (which I think is a statement we can all agree with) before presenting the following hypothesis:

Samhain is originally believed to derive from the union of the words sam, meaning "summer" and fuin meaning "fun".

This one seems hard to swallow. Northwestern Europe, the land where Samhain originated, is not the ideal locale for having "summer fun" at the end of October.

But perhaps that's because Samhain is rooted in a much older Celtic holiday, one that began in ancient Gaul.

That's a topic I'll explore in more detail in the next chapter...

3. SAMHAIN HISTORY: WHEN (AND WHERE) DID HALLOWEEN'S PREDECESSOR GET ITS START?

As I explored in the previous chapter, the October 31st/ November 1st festival was ancient Ireland's pagan New Year celebration. Samhain ("summer's end") marked the conclusion of one pastoral year and the commencement of the next.

As an ancient Celt, you would have been keenly aware that the days were noticeably shorter during the Samhain season, as if the sun itself were in retreat.

The world was darker.

The harvest, over.

Samhain was a liminal time. A time when worries spread and imaginations ran wild. So the ancient Celts did what any sensible people would do in the face of encroaching darkness:

They shined a light.

To quote Scottish scholar and folklore researcher J.A. MacCulloch:

"As the powers of growth were in danger and in eclipse in winter, men thought it necessary to assist them. As a magical aid the Samhain bonfire was chief..." (source: *The Religion of the Ancient Celts,* 1911).

These "powers", the forces of nature, really, "came to be associated with Samhain as demoniac beings," noted MacCulloch.

Hence, Samhain was a time when "[w]itches, evil-intentioned fairies, and the dead were particularly active," including "the 'malignant bird flocks' which blighted crops and killed animals, the samhanach which steals children, and Mongfind the banshee, to whom 'women and the rabble' make petitions on Samhain eve."

Spooky stuff.

And while it's clear why Samhain—and later, Halloween—became associated with death and demons and ill-intentioned fairies, what's less clear is when and where Samhain originated in the first place.

THE ORIGINS OF SAMHAIN

While the term "Samhain" is used to describe the October 31st/November 1st Celtic harvest festival as it occurred in pre-Christian Ireland, the roots of said festival undoubtedly date back not only to much earlier, but also back to the European continent.

We know this for two reasons:

1. Archaeological & Historical Evidence

Archaeological evidence—including the Coligny calendar, dated to the 2nd century CE—suggests that the Celts of ancient Gaul (roughly modern-day France) celebrated their new year at the end of summer (source: *Histoire du calendrier gaulois,* 1999, by Joseph Monard).

Calendrier de Coligny: Overview of the re-assembled tablet found in Coligny, France

The first month of the Gaulish new year was called "Samonios" in the Gaulish language, derived from the root "*samo-*," meaning summer, leading some scholars to believe that the Irish Samhain evolved from this Gaulish Samonios.

Samonios on the Coligny calendar

Medieval manuscripts, meanwhile, tell us that the Gaels—Goidelic-speaking Celts—came to Ireland via Galicia, which, for those unfamiliar, is in the Northwest of the Iberian peninsula. These were the famed, quasi-legendary Milesians, who, according to the *Annals of the Four Masters*, invaded Ireland in 1700 BCE.

"The Coming of the Sons of Miled", illustration by J. C. Leyendecker in T. W. Rolleston's Myths & Legends of the Celtic Race, *1911*

More conservative estimates place the arrival of Ireland's first Celts closer to 1000 BCE, 500 BCE, or even as late as 100 BCE. At the other end of the spectrum, some have argued the first Celts arrived in Ireland as early as 3500 BCE or even 5000 BCE.

Here's what we know for sure, according to archaeologist Holly Burton: "By the 5th century A.D., the beginning of Irish historical records, all of Ireland was Celtic speaking," (source: "The Arrival of the Celts in Ireland" *Expedition Magazine* 21.3, 1979).

2. Samhain's Spread

Regardless of when, precisely, the Gaels introduced Samhain—or at least the name for Samhain—to Ireland, the festival went on to become one of if not the most important holidays on the island. Turns out, this wasn't an isolated incident.

Just about every territory settled by—or at least heavily influenced by—the ancient continental Celts would come to celebrate a version of the same holiday on October 31st/November 1st. Those territories include the Gaelic-speaking Celtic countries (Ireland, Scotland, the Isle of Man) as well as the Brittonic-speaking Celtic countries (Wales, Cornwall, Brittany).

Britain & Ireland in the early–mid 1st millennium AD, before the founding of Anglo-Saxon kingdoms. Red (right): Celtic Britons. Blue (top right): Picts. Green (left): Gaels.

In Ireland, of course, the October 31st/November 1st holiday is Samhain. In Scotland, it's Samhuinn. And in the Isle of Man, the folk name for the festival is Hop-tu-Naa. However, it's properly called "Oie Houney" in the native Manx.

This Manx term, *Oie Houney*, may correspond to the Irish *"oidhche Samhain"* (a.k.a. *"Oíche Shamhna"*). Here's how MacCulloch explains the origin of the phrase:

"The Celtic year was not at first regulated by the solstices and equinoxes, but by some method connected with agriculture or with the seasons. Later, the year was a lunar one, and there is some evidence of attempts at synchronising solar and lunar time. But time was mainly measured by the moon, while in all calculations night preceded day. Thus *oidhche Samhain* was the night preceding Samhain (November 1st), not the following night. The usage survives in our 'sennight' and 'fortnight.'"

According to an oral history interview conducted by Culture Vannin, it's likely that Hop-tu-Naa/Oie Houney —the Manx version of Samhain—is the oldest unbroken tradition in the Isle of Man's history.

Now, on the Brythonic-/Brittonic-speaking side of the Celtic language house, the October 31st/November 1st festival is referred to not as "summer's end", but as the "calends of winter"—"calends" begin a fancy word for "the first day of."

Thus, in Wales, the Samhain-equivalent festival is called Calan Gaeaf; in Cornwall, it's Kalan Gwav; and in Brittany, it's Kalan Goañv.

Despite this difference in naming convention—"summer's end" vs. "winter's beginning"—the Britons celebrated their October 31st/November 1st festivals much in the same manner as the Gaels. Death was the central theme. Ceremonial fires were lit to guard against the coming darkness of winter. Adult beverages were consumed.

The universality of the Samhain holiday across the Celtic world suggests a common continental progenitor. Literally every one of the so-called "six Celtic nations" celebrates some variation of it. As does Galicia, the "seventh

Celtic nation," where Samhain has been translated into the Galician language (a.k.a. Gallego) as "Samaín" and is celebrated in conjunction with Magosto, the chestnut-roasting festival.

And yes, you better believe those chestnuts are roasted over an open fire.

Castañas asadas: "Roasted chestnut of All Saints' Day, a likely origin for the chestnut basis of this holiday" (source: Wikimedia Commons)

SAMHAIN'S CHRISTIANIZATION

The ubiquity of Samhain and its equivalent Celtic death holidays in Atlantic Europe no doubt caught the attention of the Catholic Church. So much so that in 835 CE, Pope Gregory III decided to "reschedule" a Christian holiday, All Saints' Day, so that it coincided with Samhain.

Up until that point, All Saints' Day—known variously as All Hallows' Day, Hallowmas, Feast of All Saints, Feast of All Hallows, and Solemnity of All Saints—was held in May. First celebrated in 609 CE, it was originally intended to honor the Virgin Mary and Christian martyrs. But when Pope Gregory III changed the date to November 1st, he also expanded the holiday to include the commemoration of all saints.

This was an obvious attempt by the Church to harness—and redirect—some of that thinking-about-dead-people energy Samhain had already generated.

"So, Celts, you've got a holiday that's all about dead people and spirits? Well, we've got a whole roster of really cool dead people you can pray to. And boy have I got a spirit for you: the Holy Spirit!"

That's what I imagine the Church's "ditch Samhain for All Saints' Day" marketing campaign would be like today.

But I digress...

It's easy to look back and say that Christianization was effective. After all, Halloween—All Hallows' Eve—is now the dominant holiday in the Western world, not Samhain.

But upon further reflection, it's clear that Halloween has become so secularized as to have lost most if not all of its Christian underpinnings. And I'd argue what we're left with, modern Halloween, has much more in common with Celtic Samhain than a Christian feast.

Indeed, as we explored in this book's introduction, nearly every Halloween tradition stems from Samhain and the imaginations of the ancient Celts.

4. SAMHAIN MYTHOLOGY: 6 STORIES THAT GIVE SAMHAIN ADDED SIGNIFICANCE

If you've been following along chapter by chapter, you already know the deal: Samhain is the Celtic New Year, marking the end of summer and the last harvest before winter. It was a time, as I've mentioned *ad nauseam*, when the barrier between our world and the world of the dead was thought to grow thin, allowing spirits to cross over.

"These supernatural spirits ruled the dead," according to author and librarian Ruth Edna Kelley (source: *The Book of Hallowe'en*, 1919). But there's more to the story than that. Because it turns out these so-called "spirits" are deeply rooted in Irish mythology.

As Kelley explains:

"There were two classes [of spirits]: the Tuatha De Danann, 'the people of the goddess Danu,' gods of light and life; and spirits of darkness and evil."

What Kelley is alluding to here is the folklorization of two mythical Irish races: the gods of Irish mythology—the Tuatha Dé Danann—who were ultimately driven underground to their folkloric fairy mounds; and the "bad guys" of Irish mythology—the Fomorians (a.k.a. Fomori)—the monstrous, semi-aquatic arch nemeses of the Tuatha Dé Danann led by Balor of the Evil Eye.

As you're about to discover, many of Irish mythology's greatest stories involve either one or both of these pantheons. And as you'll also see, many of the most significant events involving the Tuatha Dé Danann and the Fomorians took place on Samhain.

1. THE TAX

The Fomorians, John Duncan's interpretation of the sea gods of Irish mythology (1912)

If Samhain wasn't spooky enough already, with all the ghosts and demons and fairies and ghost-demon-fairies (like the banshee) hovering around... it was also tax day.

Chills.

Granted, this was back in the era of Fomorian rule, well before the Tuatha De Dannan (gods) or Milesians (Celts) arrived in Ireland. Ireland's inhabitants at the time were the Nemedians, who themselves had invaded the island, displacing a previous group (the Partholonians).

It's a whole thing.

By which I mean the subsequent invasions of Ireland—six in total by six different groups: the Cessair, the Partholónians, the Nemedians, the Fir Bolg, the Tuatha Dé Danann, and the Milesians—is a central narrative in Ireland's mythology, as detailed in the 11th-century *Lebor Gabála Érenn*, or *Book of Invasions* (a.k.a. *The Book of the Taking of Ireland*).

But I digress.

The Fomorians were raiders. Operating out of their fortress on Tory Island (off of County Donegal's northwest coast), they never settled in Ireland, but preferred instead to make life miserable for its inhabitants—whoever they happened to be at the time.

After decimating the Nemedians, the Fomorians imposed a tax. A gruesome tax. Due on Samhain.

To quote Kelley: "[T]he Fomor, sea-demons, after destroying nearly all their enemies by plagues, exacted from those remaining, as tribute, 'a third part of their corn, a third part of their milk, and a third part of their children.' This tax was paid on Samhain. It was on the week before Samhain that the Fomor landed upon Ireland. On the eve of Samhain the gods met them in the second battle of Moytura, and they were driven back into the ocean."

No, not good. Not good at all.

But somehow, in another interpretation of this Samhain myth, the tax is even worse. Two times worse, to be precise.

To quote Scottish scholar and folklore researcher J.A. MacCulloch:

"From Tory Island the Fomorians ruled Ireland, and forced the Nemedians to pay them annually on the eve of Samhain (Nov. 1st) two-thirds of their corn and milk and of the children born during the year. If the Fomorians are gods of darkness, or, preferably, aboriginal deities, the tribute must be explained as a dim memory of sacrifice offered at the beginning of winter when the powers of darkness and blight are in the ascendant," (source: *The Religion of the Ancient Celts*, 1911).

According to MacCulloch's analysis, the Fomorians were effectively the original Samhain demons. They were embodiments or manifestations of the darkness and death (especially crop death) associated with the coming winter.

Appeasing sea-demon deities of darkness required sacrifice, no doubt— perhaps at one time even human sacrifice. And later, that evolved into making offerings of food.

It could be argued that the Fomorians invented the Halloween tradition of trick-or-treating as they forced households to put out snacks. No, seriously. And, in response to the other part of the tax, maybe Nemedian parents dressed up their children in costumes on Samhain eve and sent them out so the Fomorians couldn't find them? Totally fits.

Am I reaching?

Of course.

But still.

2. THE ARRANGEMENT

Flash forward a couple of invasions and the Tuatha Dé Danann have defeated the Fir Bolg in the first Battle of Magh Tuireadh (a.k.a. the first Battle of Moytura).

The Dagda, the father of the Irish gods, also known as Eochaid Ollathair (the All-Father), is taking a well-deserved break from swinging his magical club, the Lorg Mór ("Great Staff"), which is so huge it has to be wheeled from place to place when not in use.

But even in his down-time, the Dagda is doing whatever it takes to ward off evil —even if that means bumping uglies with the most sinister member of the Tuatha Dé Danann: the Morrígan.

*Ambassadors of the Fir Bolg and Tuath Dé meeting before
the Battle of Moytura. An illustration by Stephen Reid in
T. W. Rolleston's* Myths & Legends of the
Celtic Race, *1911*

A quick reminder: the Tuatha Dé
Danann is named for the Celtic mother
goddess Danu, bringer and nurturer of
life. As mentioned in my article "What Is
Samhain?", the battle and death goddess
the Morrígan is Danu's divine opposite,

possessing "the power of destruction and the fury of slaughter."

That's according to archaeologist and academic Barry Cunliffe, who goes on to note that the "ferocious" Morrígan "could bring devastation and death" and "needed careful handling and much propitiation," (source: *Druids: A Very Short Introduction*, 2010).

Thus, to keep the Morrígan at bay, the following arrangement was struck:

"The Dagda engaged in intercourse with the Morrígan once a year on the feast of Samain, thus commanding her protection for his people for the year to come."

This is a recurring theme I see in Samhain folklore and mythology: it's a time when evil hasn't broken through... not quite yet...or at least not completely. But it's pushing up against that veil, that thinnest of membranes between worlds. So there's a lingering fear: will this be the year this whole delicate system collapses and evil is unleashed en force?

3. THE ARRIVAL

A young god walks into the court at Tara —seat of Ireland's High King—boasting of his many talents. What he does next will lead to one of Irish mythology's most famous battles.

This is the story of the "Coming of Lugh", Lugh being an Irish sun-god, cognate with the Gaulish Lugos and the Welsh Lleu.

The Evolution of a Celtic God

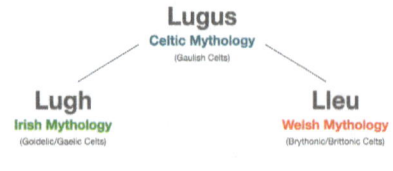

In Irish mythology, he is the son of Cian, who in turn is the son of Dian Cécht, Irish god of healing and medicine. More infamously, Lugh is also the son of Ethlinn, daughter of Balor of the Evil

Eye—leader of the Fomorians.

Fortunately for then-king Nuada of the Silver Hand, Lugh would ultimately decide to join the side of the Tuatha Dé Danann in the battle against the Fomorians. But first, Lugh had to convince the guards to let him into Tara. So he listed off all of his many skills, which included carpentry, blacksmithing, fighting, harp-playing, poetry, storytelling, magic, healing, cup-bearing, and metalworking.

But with each skill Lugh listed, the guards shook their heads. "We already have someone who can do that," they told him (paraphrasing).

Finally, Lugh responded: "Go and ask the king if he has any one man that can do all these things, and if he has, I will not ask to come into Teamhair [Tara]," (source: Irish dramatist and folklorist Lady Gregory, *Gods and Fighting Men*, 1902).

Lugh was let into Tara, where his claims were promptly put to the test. He completed all of the feats of strength and wit and musical ability leveled at him with flying colors.

I'll let Lady Gregory tell the rest:

"And when Nuada saw all the things Lugh could do, he began to think that by his help the country might get free of the taxes and the tyranny put on it by the Fomor. And it is what he did, he came down from his throne, and he put Lugh on it in his place, for the length of thirteen days, the way they might all listen to the advice he would give."

Oh, right, and what was the date of Lugh's arrival in Tara? You guessed it:

Samhain.

An altar depicting a three-faced god identified as Lugh/Lugus

For the next several years, Lugh would help the Tuatha Dé Danann prepare for a battle which would take place on another fateful Samhain. But the Samhain date has another significance as well:

Remember the aforementioned arrangement between the Dagda and the Morrígan? Well, Lugh's arrival had the potential to jeopardize it, as Lugh was not just some new god—he represented a divine paradigm shift.

To quote Cunliffe:

"There is, however, another male deity – Lug – who at first sight seems to stand aside as something different. He is the antithesis of the Dagda – young, beautiful, and pure, contrasting with the aged, ugly, grossness of the Dagda. His weapons are throwing weapons – the sling and the spear – very different to the Dagda's heavy club, and whereas the Dagda commands all knowledge, Lug is the many-skilled. One way to structure this would be to see the Lug/Dagda dichotomy as the two opposing sides of a single male deity, much as the Morrígan encompasses the oppositions of wellbeing and destruction contained within the female form. In the overarching scheme, then, the productive and destructive forces of nature confront the traditional and progressive forces in humanity."

4. THE BATTLE

On Samhain, twenty-seven years after overthrowing the Fir Bolg in the first battle of Magh Tuireadh, the Tuatha Dé Danann, weapons in hand (or, in the Dagda's case, in tow), returned to the hallowed ground of Magh Tuireadh (a.k.a. Moytura) to confront the Fomorians.

Or rather, they returned to a spot about 50 miles from the site of the original battlefield (in County Mayo) to a plain in County Sligo. But let's not get too bogged down by the details.

The second battle of Magh Tuireadh (a.k.a. Cath Tánaiste Maige Tuired) could, in modern terms, be described as a Tolkien-esque affair, complete with magical weaponry, enchanted armor, battle companions with cool names, horses with even cooler names, and heroes on horseback making dramatic entrances with their armies behind them.

No one's entrance being so dramatic, of course, as you-know-whose:

"Nuada was holding a great assembly ... they saw an armed troop coming towards them from the east, over the plain; and there was a young man in front of the troop, in command over the rest, and the brightness of his face was like the setting sun, so that they were not able to look at him because of its brightness.

"And when he came nearer they knew it was Lugh Lamh-Fada, of the Long Hand, that had come back to them, and along with him were the Riders of the Sidhe from the Land of Promise, and his own foster-brothers, the sons of Manannan, Sgoith Gleigeil, the White Flower, and Goitne Gorm-Shuileach, the Blue-eyed Spear, and Sine Sindearg, of the Red Ring, and Donall Donn-Ruadh, of the Red-brown Hair.

"Illustration of Lugh's magic spear by Harold Robert
Millar. From: Squire, Charles (n.d.), "Chapter 5: The
Gods of the Gaels", in Celtic Myth And Legend
Poetry And Romance, *London: Gresham Publishing*
Company, page 62. Originally published under the title
The Mythology of the British Islands, 1905."
(source: Wikimedia Commons)

"And it is the way Lugh was, he had
Manannan's horse, the Aonbharr, of the
One Mane, under him, that was as swift
as the naked cold wind of spring, and the

sea was the same as dry land to her, and the rider was never killed off her back.

"And he had Manannan's breast-plate on him, that kept whoever was wearing it from wounds, and a helmet on his head with two beautiful precious stones set in the front of it and one at the back, and when he took it off, his forehead was like the sun on a dry summer day.

"And he had Manannan's sword, the Freagarthach, the Answerer, at his side, and no one that was wounded by it would ever get away alive; and when that sword was bared in a battle, no man that saw it coming against him had any more strength than a woman in child-birth.

"And the troop came to where the King of Ireland was with the Tuatha de Danaan, and they welcomed one another," (source: *Gods and Fighting Men*, 1902).

Boom.

That's how you introduce the hero. (Minus that "woman in child-birth" comment, of course.)

Lugh *was* the undisputed hero of the second battle of Magh Tuireadh, killing his own grandfather—Fomorian leader, Balor of the Evil Eye—with a special slingshot projectile called the Tathlum, made by mixing the blood of toads, bears, and vipers with sea-sand and letting it harden.

Yum.

Unfortunately, Lugh was not able to deliver this fatal shot until after Balor had slayed Nuada of the Silver Hand, leader of the Tuatha Dé Danann. Thus, while the forces of goodness and light ultimately triumphed over the forces of evil and darkness—on Samhain, no less—it was a bittersweet victory.

To quote MacCulloch:

"Samhain may thus be regarded as, in origin, an old pastoral and agricultural festival, which in time came to be looked upon as affording assistance to the powers of growth in their conflict with the powers of blight. Perhaps some myth describing this combat may lurk behind the story of the battle of Mag-tured fought on Samhain between the Tuatha Dé Danann and the Fomorians. While the powers of blight are triumphant in winter, the Tuatha Déa are represented as the victors, though they suffer loss and death. Perhaps this enshrines the belief in the continual triumph of life and growth over blight and decay, or it may arise from the fact that Samhain was both a time of rejoicing for the ingathered harvest, and of wailing for the coming supremacy of winter and the reign of the powers of blight."

And MacCulloch isn't the only scholar to have drawn a connection between Samhain and the second battle of Magh Tuireadh. To quote Kelley:

"Samhain was then a day sacred to the death of the sun, on which had been paid a sacrifice of death to evil powers. Though overcome at Moytura, evil was ascendant at Samhain. Methods of finding out the will of spirits and the future naturally worked better then, charms and invocations had more power, for the spirits were near to help, if care was taken not to anger them, and due honors paid."

5. THE RAID

Events from the Táin *in a mosaic mural in Dublin by Desmond Kinney*

So far we've been dealing with Samhain myths only from the Mythological Cycle of Irish mythology—the earliest of the four cycles. Now it is time to delve into the second cycle: the Ulster Cycle, also known as the Red Branch Cycle, whose stories concern the battles and skirmishes of the Red Branch warriors, foremost among them Cú Chulainn: the hound of Cullan (a.k.a. the hound of Ulster, a.k.a. the Irish Achilles).

Arguably, Cú Chulainn is Ireland's greatest hero. Like, of all time. Ever. Even greater than the aforementioned Lugh, who, I should add, is Cú Chulainn's biological father.

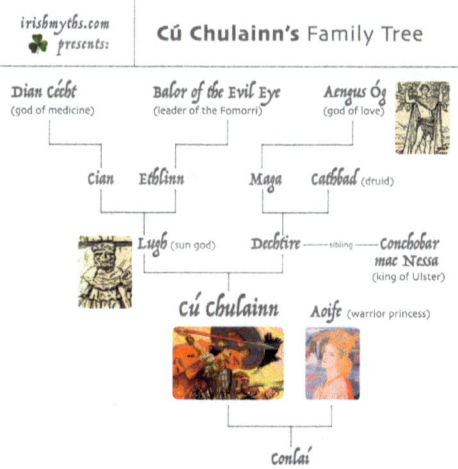

The story that really solidifies Cú Chulainn's place amongst the greats is the *Tain Bo Cualigne* (*Cattle Raid of Cooley*), an epic poem that sees Queen

Medb (a.k.a. Maeve) of Connacht attempting to capture a prize bull of Ulster. Specifically, Donn Cuailnge: "The Brown Bull of Cooley".

Finnbhennach (left) & Donn Cuailnge (right) / mural in Dublin by Desmond Kinney

See, Donn Cuailnge's brother, Finnbhennach ("The White-Horned") once belonged to Queen Medb's herd. But Finnbhennach was a chauvinist and considered being part of a woman's herd beneath him (ouch). So, he joined her husband's cattle herd (twist!). Medb's plan to capture Finnbhennach's brother— Ulster's prized bull, the Brown Bull of Cooley—is born shortly thereafter.

When does Medb launch her attack?

Ding, ding, ding.

Samhain.

And you better believe that some witchy stuff is a-brewing.

For starters, when Medb's army arrives in Ulster, all of the Red Branch knights—Ulster's champions and defenders—are incapacitated with labor pains, courtesy of a curse. In most tellings this curse is conjured by Macha, who is likely an incarnation of the Morrígan.

So it is up to the lad Cú Chulainn—only a teenager at the time—to fight off Medb's army single-handedly…

Which he does, invoking the right of single combat so he can battle each of Connacht's champions one-on-one.

It isn't easy. And the Morrígan, who is constantly shapeshifting and messing with Cú Chulainn during his fights (e.g. by turning into a beautiful woman and seducing him, by turning into an eel and biting him, etc.), doesn't make it any easier.

Macha Curses the Men of Ulster (1904) by Eleanor Hull, The Boys' Cuchulain *(Stephen Reid)*

While Maeve's decision to launch her raid on Samhain probably had more to do with strategic considerations than supernatural ones (as most cattle-raids, a common occurrence in ancient Ireland, took place in the summer), the Samhain date meant that "charms and invocations had more power," as Kelley told us in the previous section. Thus, Macha/the Morrígan were perhaps able to wield more power than usual—to the detriment of the Red Branch and Cú Chulainn.

Also, it should be noted that while Cú Chulainn took the opportunity of the raid to prove himself as a warrior, Medb still managed to steal Ulster's prize bull.

It's a bittersweet, cursed-with-labor-pains symphony. That's Samhain.

6. THE SHOWDOWN

Take all the elements of a good Samhain myth (or any Celtic myth, really)—an otherworldly foe; the testing of a young champion; a magical weapon; FIRE—put them together and you've got something approaching the story of Fionn mac Cumhail and the fire-breathing monster Aillén mac Midgna.

Fionn mac Cumhail (a.k.a. Finn McCool), a lad of just ten years—yes, you read that right, he was ten—goes marching into the court at Tara, much in the vein of Lugh, to help the high king with a problem:

For the past twenty years and change, Aillén has crossed over from the Otherworld on Samhain and burnt Tara to the ground with his fire-breath.

Fionn fighting Aillen, illustration by Beatrice Elvery in Violet Russell's Heroes of the Dawn *(1914)*

However, Fionn is about to put this streak to an end.

This story is from the Fenian Cycle of Irish mythology, FYI, which is third chronologically (after the Ulster Cycle, before the Cycle of Kings). It was originally recorded in the medieval narrative *The Boyhood Deeds of Fionn*, or *Macgnímartha Finn*.

Now, on with the show.

Aillén's secret weapon, apart from his fire-breath, is his timpán (a lyre-like stringed instrument). He is a master of the *suantraí* (lullaby) style of ancient Irish music, which he deploys, every Samhain, to put the denizens of Tara into a deep, death-like sleep.

Fionn has a solution: the Spear of Fiacha, a.k.a. Birgha (the Spit-Spear), an enchanted, venomous spear which was gifted to him by Fiacha, a member of the Fianna who once served under Fionn's father, Cumal.

"Finn Mccool Comes to Aid the Fianna" – *Fionn mac
Cumhaill meets his father's old retainers in the forests of
Connacht; illustration by Stephen Reid, from* The High
Deeds of Finn and Other Bardic Fictions of
Ancient Ireland.

Fiacha gives Fionn the spear with the
express intention that Fionn will slay
Aillén on Samhain, saving the royal
residence of Tara from destruction. In
one version of the story he even teaches
Fionn how to use the spear. In another

version, it is Fionn who figures out how to unlock the spear's power. Regardless, the outcome is the same.

During his Samhain battle with Aillén, Fionn presses the spear's blade to his own forehead and inhales its magical fumes, inoculating himself against Aillén's timpán music. Our hero is then able to slay the monster.

Fionn gives the spoils of his victory, Aillén's timpán—or in other versions, Aillén's severed head—to the High King of Ireland.

The head-gift was par for the course for the ancient Celts, who regularly kept the heads of their vanquished enemies as trophies. But this act may be seen as having even greater significance on Samhain, when the Celtic "cult of the head" was celebrated with carved turnip jack-o'-lanterns.

Now, is there any more hidden symbolism or spirituality we can attribute to this story of a boy vanquishing evil on Samhain?

One can't help but to consider that in some interpretations of Fionn's lineage, his maternal great-grandfather is Nuada of the Silver Hand, while his maternal great-grandmother is Ethlinn, daughter of Balor of the Evil Eye.

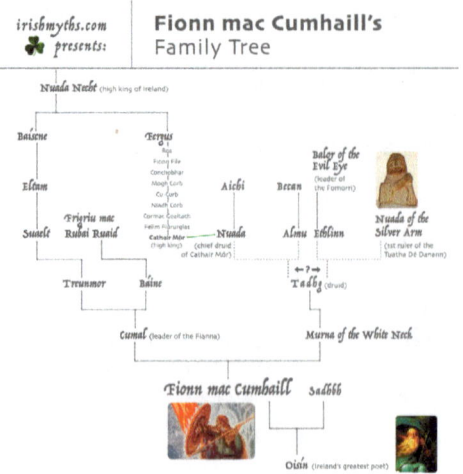

irishmyths.com presents:

Fionn mac Cumhaill's Family Tree

Which means yes, Fionn is both a descendant of the Tuatha Dé Danann and the Fomorians. A mix of good and evil.

On Samhain, he makes a choice to fight on the side of goodness, holding evil at bay.

5. WAS THERE AN IRISH GOD NAMED SAMHAIN?

FrMany of us take it for granted that Halloween, which originated with the Celtic holiday of Samhain, has been secularized to the point that people of various religious (and non-religious) backgrounds get together to celebrate it each and every year.

But as I (and many others) recently witnessed in Nathan Fielder's series *The*

Rehearsal, there is still a lot of misinformation out there about the origins of Halloween—and the origins of Samhain in particular.

Apparently, there are certain religious organizations whose members believe that Samhain originated as a Satanic holiday. Tangental to this belief is the idea that Samhain was named after a pagan god, Sam Hain, an Irish god of death.

Of course, these beliefs conflict with the historical and archaeological evidence.

First and foremost, we know who the Irish gods of death are. ("Sam Hain" isn't one of them.)

Second, most academics agree on the etymology of Samhain: it means "Summer's End". It's not the name of a person, it's the name of a day. But not just a day. A Celtic cross-quarter day. A day equidistant between the autumnal equinox and the winter solstice. Samhain was the Celtic New Year—the end of one pastoral year and the start of the next.

In modern Irish, the entire month of November is now known as Samhain, a tribute to the important cultural festival that took place on the evening of October 31st into November 1st.

This calendrical tribute is especially fitting given that the Irish word Samhain potentially shares the Celtic root *"samo-"*, meaning summer, with the Gaulish "Samonios", the first month of the Gaulish new year.

All this to say: Samhain is not, and never was, the name of some Satanic death deity.

So why do so many people think that it is?

BLAME IT ALL ON CHARLES VALLANCEY

General Charles Vallancey came to Ireland in the late 1760s to assist with a British military survey. Little did he know at the time that Ireland would become his adopted homeland (much in the vein of St. Patrick), and for the next several decades Vallancey would dedicate himself to documenting the island's many stories and traditions.

As a documentarian and antiquarian, it can be argued that Vallancey's contributions to preserving Irish folklore and mythology were invaluable. At one point he even came into possession of the *Great Book of Lecan* (*Leabhar Mór Leacáin*)—a medieval Irish manuscript written between 1397 and 1418—which he donated to the Royal Irish Academy.

But for all of his good intentions, Vallancey suffered from an overactive imagination. And that is perhaps putting it lightly.

According to the *Quarterly Review*, Vallancey "wrote more nonsense than any man of his time."

Irish antiquarian George Petrie described Vallancey's reasonings as "rambling," his style as "obscure," and his hypotheses as being "of a visionary nature."

Finally, the Edinburgh Review offered the following summary of Vallancey's academic output:

"To expose the continual error of his theory will not cure his inveterate disease. It can only excite hopes of preventing infection by showing that he has reduced that kind of writing to absurdity, and raised a warning monument to all antiquaries and philologians that may succeed him," (source: Alfred Webb's *A Compendium of Irish Biography*, 1878).

So, what exactly did Vallancey write to earn such scorn?

Welp, in his 1786 book, *A Vindication of the Ancient History of Ireland*, he argued that the Irish people originated in Armenia, and that Irish god Nuada of the Silver Hand, leader of the Tuatha Dé Danann, was actually that same person as the Iranian prophet Zoroaster, founder of the religious movement Zoroastrianism.

In that same book, Vallancey nonchalantly—and without evidence—described a god from Irish mythology by the name of "Saman", writing: "The Irish deity Saman was supposed to be the judge of departed souls; at his direction they were condemned to be punished…"

Vallancey equated this (alleged) Irish death deity "Saman" (a.k.a. Samain/ Samhain) with Asuman of Persian mythology, referring to both as "the Angel of death."

An artistic depiction of the angel of death. Painted in 1881 by Evelyn De Morgan, née Pickering

So one can see how a Satan-fearing Christian might come to conflate Vallancey's Samhain the god with Samhain the Celtic festival, assigning the god's devilish reputation to his eponymous day.

But by all accounts, Vallancey's god of Samhain was a pure fabrication. There is no description of such a character to be found anywhere in medieval Irish literature.

That being said, *some* of the literature *does* mention a (minor) character named Samhain, who may or may not have been a god...

WILL THE REAL (MYTHICAL) SAMHAIN PLEASE STAND UP?

In his *A Dictionary of Irish Mythology* (1987), historian Peter Berresford Ellis gives the following brief biography of a god named Samhain:

"Brother of Cian and Goibhniu who was looking after Cian's magical cow, Glas

Gaibhnenn, when Balor of the Evil Eye, disguised as a little red-haired boy, tricked him into parting with it. He was obviously one of the gods but his role does not seem clearly defined although one of the four major Celtic feasts appears to have been named after him."

The story of the god Samhain, it turns out, is really just the setup to a well-known Irish myth, the story of Cian and Ethlinn (a.k.a. Ethniu), which sees Cian journey to Tory Island, home of the Fomorians, to recover his cow. In the process he ends up getting intimate with Balor's daughter, Ethlinn, jumpstarting a familial line that would include the likes of Lugh, Irish sun-god and god of many talents, and Cú Chulainn, arguably Ireland's greatest champion.

Samhain's role in these proceedings is minimal. It's a bit part. And his character doesn't even appear in every telling of the story. To quote pagan author and educator Patti Wigington:

Cian Finds Balor's Daughter, drawing by H. R. Millar, c. 1905. From Charles Squire's popular book Celtic Myth And Legend, Poetry And Romance, *originally published under the title* The Mythology of the British Islands *(1905)*

"Although Samain (alternately, Sawen or Mac Samthainn) appears in a few versions of the story, depending on who translated it and when, he does not appear in all of them. Regardless, even in the ones that do include him, he is a very obscure and minor character, and certainly not a deity. In fact, most lists of Celtic language variants don't mention him at all. He's just not that important— he's a guy who lost his brother's magical cow, not the 'lord of the dead'," (source: LearnReligions.com).

Wigington also notes that Lady Charlotte Guest's translation of *The Mabinogion*, a compendium of Welsh myths, is one of the few sources that adds "Samaín" as a third brother to Goibniu and Cian, giving him the role of a (not very good) sheep-watcher.

Weirdly, I wasn't able to find this reference in the version of Guest's translation I looked at. I did find the Welsh equivalent of the Cian and Ethlinn story—"Kilhwch and Olwen"—but apart, perhaps, from a single mention of the name "Siawn" (nestled amongst a long list of other names), Samhain does not feature in the story at all.

He is an elusive fellow, this Samhain. And exceptionally ambiguous, his divine status ranging from "certainly not a deity" (according to Wigington) to "obviously one of the gods" (according to Ellis).

Divinity aside, it's widely agreed upon that the Samhain of Irish mythology is a poorly defined character—we simply do not know much about him. So the suggestion that Samhain, the festival, one of the most important holidays on the Celtic calendar, was named after this dude seems almost laughable.

Surely, it was the other way around: There was probably some medieval scribe, perhaps inspired by the season he was writing in, who added the character as a gag. Need someone to blame for losing the main character's prized cattle? Make the culprit an incarnation of "summer's end", the great turning point from days of sunshine and growth to days of darkness and death.

But hey, that's just a theory— hopefully one that isn't nonsense. And I pray my reasonings weren't too rambling and my style not too obscure.

6. MEET THE IRISH GOD(S) OF DEATH: THE MORRÍGAN, DONN, AND BILÉ

The Irish have a special relationship with death, I think it's safe to say. (Or is it better to say that death has a special relationship with them?)

To quote Scottish journalist Kevin Toolis, you'd be hard-pressed to find a country other than Ireland "where the dying…the living, the bereaved and the dead still openly share the world and remain bound together in the Irish wake." A place where "death, in its very ordinariness, is no stranger," (source: *The Guardian*).

Historically, the Gaelic / Goidelic Celts of Ireland likely held a similar viewpoint. Long before the rise of Christianity, Celtic druids preached that the human soul was eternal. In death, one "simply" moved into a different plane of existence, a different realm (i.e., the Otherworld).

image created with Dall-E mini using the prompt "Irish god of death"

Irish myths tell us that the barriers between the land of the living and the Otherworld are not always solid. At certain times, like Samhain, the walls between worlds become permeable. (Just ask Fionn mac Cumhaill, the Irish hero who fought a fire-breathing monster from the Otherworld on Samhain. But I digress).

In other stories—myth, legend, folklore, and fairytale alike—Death is anthropomorphized. And in author and librarian Ruth Edna Kelley's account of Samhain's ancient origins, it is "the lord of death" who hosts Samhain, in a sense, collecting souls and passing judgment.

And I quote:

"They believed that on the last night of the old year (October 31st) the lord of death gathered together the souls of all those who had died in the passing year and had been condemned to live in the bodies of animals, to decree what forms they should inhabit for the next twelve months. He could be coaxed to give lighter sentences by gifts and prayers," (source: *The Book of Hallowe'en*, 1919).

Oh, right, forgot to mention: lots of people in Irish mythology get turned into animals. It happens all the time. Definitely more than you'd think.

Étaín transforms into a bejeweled, music-making fly.

Tuan Mac Cairell transforms into a salmon.

Lir's children turn into swans.

In later legends, St. Patrick transforms into a deer.

And we can't forget about Irish werewolves (a.k.a. wolfwalkers), like the daughters of Airitech and the man-wolves of Ossory.

The takeaway here:

It makes sense the Irish gods would have amongst their ranks someone (re: a lord of death) who could manage…all that.

But who is he?

Or, should I really be asking, who is she?

1. THE MORRÍGAN

The Morrígan was the "major goddess of war, of death and slaughter," according to historian Peter Berresford Ellis. "She embodied all that was perverse and horrible among the supernatural powers" (source: *A Dictionary of Irish Mythology*, 1987).

Yikes.

Also known as the Morrigu (or Mór-Ríoghain in modern Irish), her name most likely means "great queen", but she's also earned the epitaphs "the crow of battle" and "supreme war goddess".

As a triune goddess, the Morrígan manifested as three separate personalities or incarnations, usually Badb, Macha, and Nemain. However, in author and scholar Charles Squire's account, there are five personalities total, all with different "responsibilities", if you will. And I quote:

"Of these warlike goddesses there were five—Fea, the 'Hateful', Nemon, the 'Venomous', Badb, the 'Fury', Macha, a personification of 'battle', and, over all of them, the Morrígú, or 'Great Queen'.

Detail of Battle Crow from "Cú Chulainn riding his chariot into battle" by Joseph Christian Leyendecker (1874 – 1951)

"This supreme war-goddess of the Gaels, who resembles a fiercer Herê, perhaps symbolized the moon, deemed by early races to have preceded the sun, and worshipped with magical and cruel rites.

"She is represented as going fully armed, and carrying two spears in her hand. As with Arês and Poseidon in the

'Iliad', her battle-cry was as loud as that of ten thousand men. Wherever there was war, either among gods or men, she, the great queen, was present, either in her own shape or in her favourite disguise, that of a 'hoodie' or carrion crow," (source: *The Mythology Of The British Islands: An Introduction to Celtic Myth, Legend, Poetry, and Romance*, 1905).

Now, folklorist and professor Juilene Osbourne-McKnight interprets the Morrígan godhead a little bit differently, calling Macha, "goddess of war"; Banbh, "goddess of carrion"; and Nemhain, "goddess of panic and chaos" (source: *The Story We Carry in our Bones*, 2015).

Regardless of the exact roles/natures of the individual sub-goddesses, it's hard to ignore that the triune or tripartite iteration of the Morrígan is the one that caught on, and the one that continues to flourish in pop culture interpretations.

Heck, I wrote a short story for *Neon Druid: An Anthology of Urban Celtic Fantasy* (2018) that depicts the Morrígan as three crows sitting on a telephone wire.

(Original, I know.)

Apparently some other writers have explored the Morrígan triad as well. To quote Osbourne-McKnight:

"So powerful is this dark trinity that they show up as the Weird Sisters in Shakespeare's *Macbeth* and later, conflated into one woman, they vie for power as Morgan Le Fay in the Arthurian myths."

No, this wouldn't be the first time Celtic mythology inspired Shakespeare (e.g., King Lear is based on the sea-god Lir) or Arthurian Legend (e.g., the story of the Green Knight is based on the Irish myth "Bricriu's Feast", which features a headless giant).

But I digress.

The question I'm really interested in is as follows:

Is the Morrígan really the Irish goddess of death? Or is she, more narrowly, the Irish goddess of death *in battle*?

Because here's the thing: Nearly every early account of the Morrígan has her witnessing, participating in, or dealing with the aftermath of a battle. Which in a way makes sense, given that, you know… lots of people died during battle. Including —and especially—in Irish mythology.

To her credit, I guess, the Morrígan fights on the side of the Tuatha Dé Danann—the Irish gods, often portrayed as "the good guys"—during both battles of Magh Tuireadh (Moytura). On Samhain, after the second battle of Magh Tuireadh, the Morrígan—with the help of the Irish god of love, Aengus Og— drives the last remaining Fomorians out of Ireland (the Fomorians being an invading race of supernatural monsters, a group once led by Balor of the Evil Eye).

The Morrígan also gives a speech after the Tuatha Dé Danann's historic victory, which sounds nice…until you consider that she's essentially celebrating all of the death that had just occurred. To quote Irish dramatist and folklorist Lady Augusta Gregory:

"And after the battle was won, and the bodies were cleared away, the Morrigu gave out the news of the great victory to the hosts and to the royal heights of

Ireland and to its chief rivers and its invers, and it is what she said: 'Peace up to the skies, the skies down to earth, the earth under the skies; strength to every one.'

"And as to the number of men that fell in the battle, it will not be known till we number the stars of the sky, or flakes of snow, or the dew on the grass, or grass under the feet of cattle, or the horses of the Son of Lir in a stormy sea," (source: *Gods and Fighting Men*, 1905).

Oh, right, almost forgot to mention: immediately following her recital of that innocent-sounding poem, the Morrígan made the following prophecy. To quote Squire:

"[S]he foretold the approaching end of the divine age, and the beginning of a new one in which summers would be flowerless and cows milkless and women shameless and men strengthless, in which there would be trees without fruit and seas without fish, when old men would give false judgments and legislators make unjust laws, when warriors would betray one another, and men would be thieves, and there would be no more virtue left in the world."

I mean… she nailed it. Right?

Moving on.

"In commemoration of the 1916 Easter Rising, a statue depicting the death of the mythical hero Cúchulainn sculpted by Oliver Sheppard in 1911 is displayed in the front window of the GPO."
(photo & caption credit: Jennifer Boyer, Flickr)

The Morrígan's favorite form to take on the battlefield was that of a crow or raven. In some stories, the Morrígan and her component goddesses would hover above soldiers, cursing them with "battle madness." This is the same affliction seen in the quasi-legendary figure Suibhne Geilt (Frenzied Sweeney) and other Celtic Wild Men.

Notably, the Morrígan tormented Cú Chulainn, arguably the greatest hero from Irish mythology, and had a front-row seat to the desecration of his corpse. As Ellis explains:

"Having first tried to incite Cuchulainn to make love to her, she [the Morrígan] fought with him and he managed to wound her. For this his fate was sealed. When he was eventually killed she settled on his shoulder in triumph in the form of a crow and watched while a beaver drank his blood."

Don't read too much into the symbolism of that one.

Just kidding, you absolutely should!

Because what the essence of the Morrígan really boils down to is the power of the sacred female.

Stick with me for a second...

Danu, another triple goddess, the one who gives the Tuatha Dé Danann their name, is a Celtic mother goddess. She's nurturing, life-giving. The Morrígan is Danu's dark reflection.

"The Paps of Dana - Called after the goddess Danu or Anu, these are on the Cork/Kerry border near Rathmore" (source: Wikimedia Commons)

As archaeologist and academic Barry Cunliffe explains:

"The female power was a goddess of the earth and of water — springs and rivers and lakes. She was a mother goddess controlling fertility and productivity, providing nourishment for the people and presiding over the seasons and the seasonal feasts: her very abundance was sometimes expressed by her triple form. But she also had within her the power of destruction and the fury of slaughter — the opposites of nurture and fertility — could bring devastation and death.

"In this dangerously unstable form she appears in the tales as the ferocious Morrígan, who needed careful handling and much propitiation…

"The Dagda engaged in intercourse with the Morrígan once a year on the feast of Samain, thus commanding her protection for his people for the year to come," (source: *Druids: A Very Short Introduction*, 2010).

So there we have it. Not only does Cunliffe clearly distinguish the Morrígan as a death goddess—the opposite of the nurturing, life-giving mother goddess, Danu—but he also provides yet another association of the Morrígan with Samhain, the ultimate Irish celebration of the dead.

Still, I'd argue that the Irish myths (or at least the earliest recorded versions of them) present death as more of the Morrígan's side hustle, whereas her main focus has always been battles: inciting them, fighting in them, and celebrating them and all their macabre details—death included.

That doesn't mean, however, that the Irish pantheon is without a true god of death.

2. DONN

Let's get this out of the way.

Yes, historian Peter Berresford Ellis describes Donn as an "Irish god of the dead", which, naturally, makes him...

Donn of the Dead.

Shall we continue?

Here's Ellis' full definition:

"Irish god of the dead whose abode is at Tech Duinn (House of Donn) which is placed on an island off the south-west of Ireland. The house is the assembly place of the dead before they begin their journey to the Otherworld. In modern folklore Donn is associated with shipwrecks and sea storms and sometimes equated with the Dagda and Bilé. In some versions he is said to be the son of Midir the Proud. More often than not he is confused with the eldest son of Milesius."source: *A Dictionary of Irish Mythology*, 1987).

There's a lot to digest there, but if you're familiar with the ancient Mediterranean polytheistic religions, what's immediately striking is that this fellow

Donn ticks many of the same "death god" boxes as Hades, Pluto, and Dis Pater.

Donn is responsible for guiding souls from the land of the living to the land of the dead.

Sound familiar?

"Orpheus before Pluto and Proserpina (1605), by Jan Brueghel the Elder."
(source: Wikimedia Commons)

As professor and Irish folklorist Dáithí Ó hÓgáin explains:

"One is struck here by the resemblance to the Greek lore of Pluto and the ferrying of souls across the river

Styx. The similarity may be explained as a common ancient tradition concerning the dead which had come down to both Greek and Celts but…it seems more sensible to regard it as having originated in general Greek influence. Since the emphasis in these death-beliefs was on the imagery of the west, it is not surprising that the lore was further extended to the westernmost island of Celtdom, Ireland itself," (source: *The Sacred Isle: Belief and Religion in Pre-Christian Ireland*, 1999).

Ó hÓgáin goes on to describe Donn as a "lord of death", while noting that the god's name is derived from the Celtic *dhuosno-*, meaning the "dark" or "black" one.

Donn's island, Tech Duinn, is in reality little more than a rock (now known as Bull Rock) situated off the coast of the Beara peninsula. But for centuries that rock inspired fear in the minds of the ancient Irish. (Then again, given what we know of Irish attitudes toward death, perhaps it didn't.)

"Bull Rock, off the southwest coast of Ireland, is often identified with Teach Duinn (the House of Donn)" (source: Wikimedia Commons)

Regardless, medieval manuscripts suggest that Donn, Irish god of the dead, was a well-respected—if not well-worshipped—deity in ancient Ireland. To quote Ó hÓgáin:

"The general cult of Donn as god of the dead must have been widely known in Ireland. Varied references in the literature as early as the 8th century AD show that the belief had been long established. One such allusion, from Ulster, is to a departed warrior returning from the realm of the dead in the House of Donn in the southwest. In another text of the same period, with Leinster provenance, a prophecy is given concerning a group of heroes to the effect that 'death will defeat them on the morning ebb towards the House of Donn'.

"In the same text, three red horsemen appear as an omen of death, and they announce: 'We ride the horses of toothless Donn from the tumuli, although we are alive we are dead!' Donn is here a personification of the elders buried in the tumuli, which illustrates the physical aspect of funerary practice."

A purely mythological figure, Donn the death god would later become conflated with the quasi-legendary Donn son of Milesius.

As Ó hÓgáin explains:

"Medieval Irish texts describe the 'belief of the heathen' to the effect that souls go there to Donn, and in the pseudo-history Donn is euhemerised as one of the leaders of the Gaelic people when they came to Ireland. We read of this pseudo-historical Donn, however, that he was not destined to reach the shore of Ireland, but was drowned near the rock which bears his name."

The Gaelic people to which Ó hÓgáin refers, of course, are the Milesians, namesake of Donn's dad Milesius (a.k.a. Míl Espáine). Originating from what is now modern Spain, the Milesians were the final invaders/settlers of ancient Ireland. They were the ones who defeated the Tuatha Dé Danann and sent them underground to their tumuli.

Donn was an important Milesian military commander and the eldest of Milesius' eight sons. He seemed like a character fated for a heroic life, yet in every account of Donn's deeds during the Milesian invasion of Ireland, shit always hits the fan. To quote Ellis:

"[W]hen he was greeted by the goddess Eire, who asked that the islands might take her name, he paid her scant respect. She foretold his doom. The Milesians put the sea again and Manannan Mac Lir caused a great storm to blow up.

"In one version Donn goes aloft to spy out the land and falls into the sea. Another version says he asked his brothers to bury him on an island off the mainland; they did, and here his tradition and that of Donn [Irish god of the dead] became intermixed."

A god of death. A god of the dead. A god associated with drownings and shipwrecks. A god who metaphorically "ferries" souls to their post-life destinations. For an Irish god of the dead, Donn is very... Mediterranean. More Greek or Roman, really, than Celtic —something I alluded to earlier.

It's hard not to think that the Christian scribes who first put Donn's tales down in ink took some liberties. They're the same scribes who introduced chariots to Irish mythology, after all.

(Meanwhile, there is no archaeological record of the ancient Irish ever having used chariots. But I digress...)

What if, as Ellis suggested, Donn is actually an offshoot or iteration of a much older Celtic god—a god who originated in ancient Gaul?

It is time, methinks, to introduce you, dear reader, to Bilé.

3. BILÉ

Call him Bilé. Call him Belenus or Belenos. Call him Bel or Beli or Bal or Baal. Just don't call him the belle of the ball, because this Celtic god ain't no pretty princess; he's the homecoming king of the dead.

Sorry, I don't know what I was doing there. But here's the important stuff:

Bilé, Irish god of death, is the Gaelic/Goidelic iteration of a much older Celtic god who is often referred to as Bel or Belinos in the Brythonic tradition. He is the namesake of the Celtic feast day Beltane, which was—and among some groups, still is—celebrated on May Eve and May 1st.

"Bonfire at the Beltane Fire Festival 2019, Calton Hill, Edinburgh. The reunited May Queen and Green Man face the fire, while dancers stop to raise their arms to heaven." (source: Wikimedia Commons)

In some ancient manuscripts Bilé is portrayed as "Father of Gods and Men", a role usually reserved for the Dagda. Bilé is also sometimes paired with the aforementioned Celtic mother goddess Danu (a.k.a. Dana a.k.a. Anu a.k.a. Ana), who was, according to author and scholar Charles Squire, "The most ancient divinity of whom we have any knowledge." Here's Squire's profile of Danu's husband:

"Her husband is never mentioned by name, but one may assume him, from British analogies, to have been Bilé, known to Gaelic tradition as a god of Hades, a kind of Celtic Dis Pater from whom sprang the first men. Danu herself probably represented the earth and its fruitfulness, and one might compare her with the Greek Demeter," (source: *The Mythology Of The British Islands*, 1905).

In case you had any doubts, Bilé was not some abstract or metaphorical lord of death, but an ancient god, in the richest sense of the world, with a strong cult that stretched across Northwestern Europe.

To quote Ellis:

"This deity had a profound influence throughout the ancient Celtic world, apparently as god of both life and death. There are many places throughout Europe named after him. In London, for example, Belinos' Gate has come down to modern times as Billingsgate.

"His name is also to be found in personal names such as that of one of the most notable kings of Britain before the Roman invasion — Cunobelinus. The Celtic form is Cunobel — the Hound of Bel. In 5BC the Romans regarded

Cunobelinus as High King of Britain. William Shakespeare has given him greater fame as *Cymbeline*."

Ellis also notes that in some Irish texts, Bilé is euhemerized (I love that word) as the father of the aforementioned Milesius.

Remember Donn from the previous section, the Irish god of the dead who was sometimes reimagined as the quasi-historical son of Milesius? Welp, consider the implication there: Bilé is the quasi-historical *father* of Milesius, making him Donn's grandfather, and clearly establishing Bilé as the original, more senior Celtic god of death.

Oh, and here's something I failed to mention earlier: Remember how the Milesians, Donn and Milesius and Bilé included, all come from Spain? Welp, in Irish mythology, "Spain" is synonymous with the Land of the Dead. To quote author and scholar Charles Squire:

"Beli is the British equivalent of the Gaelic Bilé, the universal Dis Pater who sent out the first Gaels from Hades to take possession of Ireland." source: The

Mythology Of The British Islands: And Introduction to the Celtic Myth, Legend, Poetry, and Romance (1905)

Catch that? Bilé and the rest of the Gaels who invaded Ireland are described as coming "from Hades."

But herein lies the mystery:

Why is this obvious god of death, Bilé, described in Classical accounts as also being the source of human life? To quote Squire again:

"Caesar tells us, in his too short account of the Gauls, that they believed themselves to be sprung from Dis Pater, the god of the underworld. In the Gaelic mythology Dis Pater was called Bilé, a name which has for root the syllable bel, meaning 'to die'.

"The god Beli in British mythology was no doubt the same person, while the same idea is expressed by the same root in the name of Balor, the terrible Fomor whose glance was death."

Yes, lots of death. But also, the ancient Gauls "believed themselves to be sprung" from Bilé.

What gives?

Well, for one, the Land of the Dead isn't the same as hell. It isn't all fire and brimstone. Instead, as historian J.A. MacCulloch explains:

"In Celtic belief the underworld was probably a fertile region and a place of light, nor were its gods harmful and evil," (source: *The Religion of the Ancient Celts*, 1911).

But apart from the potentially fertile nature of the Celtic underworld, it's likely that Bilé was actually the dark reflection of the Dagda or some other "positive" male deity, just as the Morrígan was the dark reflection of Danu.

And while Bilé, the Father deity's dark incarnation, wasn't well-known for playing a role in the life-giving side of things, he was, indeed, crucial to the circle of life nonetheless.

After all, death begets life. And the most fertile soil is that which is rich with the remains of the once-living.

So yes, in a way, that makes Bilé a spiritual father to humankind, just as it makes the Morrígan a spiritual mother.

image created with Dall-E mini using the prompt "Irish god of death"

7. JACK-O'-LANTERN ORIGINS: A TALE OF TURNIPS, SAMHAIN, AND SEVERED HEADS

I admit it. I am one of *those* people — a person whose favorite holiday is Halloween, who still dresses up every year despite being in my thirties, and who loves, loves, LOVES, carving pumpkins. Maybe too much.

A couple of years ago, after watching far too many pumpkin carving competition shows on TV, I decided I was done with templates, done with two-dimensional jack-o'-lantern designs. I bought my first "professional" carving kit, complete with wood-handled sculpting tools. The following year, I upgraded to an even more professional carving kit. My results have been...meh. (See for yourself.)

But I'm not giving up! I am admittedly addicted to the art of pumpkin carving, and more specifically, to the art of creating jack-o'-lanterns with big ole teeth and grotesque expressions. For years, I believed it was my Massachusetts upbringing that instilled this passion in me. Growing up a stone's throw away from Salem (of witch trials fame),

Halloween was always a big deal.

But what if my love of jack-o'-lanterns goes deeper than that?

What if it's in my blood?

THE IRISH ORIGINS OF THE JACK-O'-LANTERN

Listen, my children, and you shall hear, of the midnight meddling of Stingy Jack, from whom the jack-o'-lantern derives its name. Or so the story goes.

Here's the most common version of the 18th-century Irish folktale:

A grumpy blacksmith by the name of Stingy Jack invites the devil for a drink but refuses to pay (hence, the "stingy" descriptor). He convinces the devil to shape-shift into a coin to cover the tab. But when the devil obliges, Jack sticks the coin in his pocket. And much to the devil-coin's dismay, there is a silver cross in that pocket, preventing him from returning to his original form. A deal is struck. Jack sets the devil free and, in return, the devil agrees A) to bar Jack from entering hell when he dies, and B) to leave Jack alone for a year.

A quick aside: This seems like a bad deal. And it is a bad deal—because guess what? A year later, the devil comes back to mess with Jack. Only Jack is ready for him. He convinces the devil to climb a tree so he might enjoy a delicious piece of fruit. Once the devil is up in the tree, Jack carves a cross into the trunk. The devil can't come down. Another (bad) deal is struck, although this one does have the advantage of being slightly less bad than the previous one. Jack frees the devil in exchange for ten years of peace.

Jack dies. (Don't be sad. He was an A-hole.) The devil, true to his word, refuses to let Jack into hell. God, meanwhile, refuses to let Jack into heaven. So, what is Jack's fate? To wander forever in eternal darkness, of course. But because the devil is not totally heartless (wait…), he tosses Jack a lump of burning coal from hell so he can have a bit of light. Jack carves out a turnip and sticks the coal inside, creating a lantern. Hence, "Jack of the Lantern," which is later shortened to "Jack O'Lantern."

Photo by Colton Sturgeon on Unsplash

The rest, as they say, is folklore.

By which I mean: There's a lot more to the story.

For starters, there's the beginning of the story, which most sources (the *Irish Times* notwithstanding) neglect. In it, Jack, acting out of character, helps an old man on the side of the road. Twist! The old man is an angel in disguise. The angel, who is clearly a fan of *One Thousand and One Nights*, grants Jack three wishes. And this is where Jack's true colors (and lack of imagination) begin to shine through.

Wish #1: anyone who sits in Jack's chair will be stuck to the spot.

Wish #2: anyone who takes a bough from Jack's sycamore tree will be stuck to the spot.

Wish #3: anyone who borrows Jack's tools will be stuck to the spot.

The angel reluctantly grants these wishes, but he makes a mental note that this Jack fellow, when the time comes, should not be allowed into heaven. Eventually, the devil comes to claim Jack, but as we already know, that plan does not go swimmingly. Granted, things don't turn out too swell for ole Jackie boy either. To quote the *Irish Times*:

"It's fitting that a character trapped in an earthly purgatory should become the lasting symbol of Halloween, a time when people are as wont to offer a 'trick' as a 'treat'. The character of Jack, a figure who doesn't fit into heaven or hell, is unusually complex for a figure from a folk tale."

This begs the question:

How are we supposed to feel about Stingy Jack? Should we be satisfied that this mean-spirited blacksmith got his comeuppance? Or, like the talkative Irish uncle quoted in an 1836 issue of the *Dublin Penny Journal* — a man who claims to have seen Jack with his own eyes — should we pity the jack-o'-lantern's namesake?

"If you knew the sufferings of that forsaken craythur, since the time the poor sowl was doomed to wandher, with a lanthern in his hand, on this cowld earth, without rest for his foot, or shelter for his head, until the day of judgment… oh, it 'ud soften the heart of stone to see him as I once did, the poor old dunawn, his feet blistered and bleeding, his poneens (rags) all flying about him, and the rains of heaven beating on his ould white head," (source: *The Irish Times*).

BOGGED DOWN BY THE DETAILS: THE ORIGINAL MEANING OF "JACK-O'-LANTERN"

So, case closed, right? We carve scary faces into vegetables on Halloween because an 18th-century Irish folk antihero once shoved a hell-coal into a turnip. Makes perfect sense. The jack-o'-lantern is a symbol of Stingy Jack's suffering. It's the perfect decoration for commemorating this awful, crafty man.

Or…not.

Because another interpretation holds that the purpose of creating jack-o'-

lanterns is not to celebrate Stingy Jack, but to protect oneself from him. To quote journalist Kayla Hertz (writing for IrishCentral):

"This legend is why people in Ireland and Scotland began to make their own versions of Jack's lantern by carving grotesque faces into turnips, mangelwurzels, potatoes, and beets, placing them beside their homes to frighten away Stingy Jack and other wandering evil spirits and travelers."

If both of these explanations feel a bit tenuous, it's because…they are. The truth is, the story of Stingy Jack was not invented to explain the origin of carved vegetable lanterns (which, as we'll explore later, go back thousands of years). Instead, the story was invented to explain a different phenomenon altogether: *ignis fatuus.*

Also known as will-o'-the-wisps, fairy lights, fool's fire, and—yes—jack-o'-lanterns, *ignis fatuus* refers to the incredibly eerie (but entirely natural) flickering of lights that occurs over peat bogs and marshlands. It's caused by the combustion of gases that are released from decomposing organic matter.

Will-o-the-wisp and snake by Hermann Hendrich 1823
(source: Wikimedia Commons)

Remember that talkative Irish uncle quoted in the previous section? He told his Stingy Jack story while gazing out at a peat bog, observing the *ignis fatuus*. That's the explanation he gave for what he was seeing. And at the time, it was a common one.

According to Nathan Mannion, senior curator of Dublin's Irish Emigration Museum, the *ignis fatuus* often seemed like "a floating flame that would move away from travelers." He goes on to say:

"If you were to try to follow the light, you could go into a sinkhole or bog, or drown. People thought it was Jack of the Lantern, a lost soul, or a ghost," (source: *National Geographic*).

To make matters even more convoluted, there is another possible origin for the term "jack-o'-lantern," one that eschews ghosts and devils and flaming bog farts and replaces them with something far more mundane: night watchmen. You see, in 17th-century Britain, "Jack" was a common catch-all for someone whose name you didn't know (sort of like the "John Doe" of its time). So an anonymous night watchman would sometimes be called a "Jack of the Lantern," or "Jack O'Lantern."

Add to this the 18th-century tradition out of Worcestershire, England known as the "Hoberdy's Lantern," which could be made by hollowing out a turnip, carving a face on the outside, and sticking a candle inside, and it's possible that the jack-o'-lantern is actually a British innovation.

Gasp! I can hear my Irish great-grandfather rolling in his grave— assuming he isn't roaming the eternal darkness of an earthly purgatory (one can never be sure).

That being said, the Irish origin for the jack-o'-lantern is still widely held by scholars and historians. And the main reason for that has to do with the Emerald Isle's Celtic history.

THE CELTIC CONNECTION: SAMHAIN AND THE CULT OF THE HEAD

In Celtic enclaves of northern Europe (e.g. Ireland, Scotland, Wales, the Isle of Man, Cornwall, Brittany) the carving of human faces into round fruits and vegetables has been going on for thousands of years. It is a tradition, according to our pal Mannion of the Irish Emigration Museum, that likely evolved from the Celtic custom of head veneration, wherein the severed heads of one's enemies were taken as war trophies.

One needs only to peruse the myths of ancient Ireland to see the significance that was placed on heads. (Not, like, literally placed on top of heads... you know what I mean.) For example, there's the story of the Ulster hero Cúchulainn, the Hound of Culann, who returned from his first-ever battle with three heads hanging from his chariot, as well as "nine heads in one hand and ten in the other, and these he brandished at the hosts in token of his valor and prowess." Meanwhile, in "The Destruction of Da Derga's Hostel," the warrior Conall pours water into the mouth of the High King of Ireland Conaire Mór's severed head—and the head thanks him.

"Cuchulain in Battle" by Joseph Christian Leyendecker (1911), via T. W. Rolleston's Myths and Legends of the Celtic Race *(source: Wikimedia Commons)*

History confirms this Celtic obsession with the head. Ancient historians Livy and Diodorus Siculus both recount instances of Celtic warriors hanging the severed heads of their slain foes from the necks of their horses. Siculus further notes that especially distinguished foes were given the royal treatment: their heads were embalmed in cedar oil and displayed with pride to visitors. This practice is also reflected in the ancient Irish tradition of creating "brain-balls," wherein the brains of enemies were hardened with lime and used as slingshot projectiles.

Lovely.

So why were heads so important to ancient Celtic peoples, including the Irish? To quote historian Peter Berresford Ellis:

"The ancient Irish revered the human head as, indeed, did all ancient Celtic societies. It was in the head and not in the heart that they seemed to locate the souls of men and women...Archaeological finds give full corroboration to this cult," (source: *A Dictionary of Irish Mythology*, 1987).

Image of stone and other balls found in irish dolmens. a) Coralline ball b) proposed Brain Ball c) proposed worn Brain Ball (source: Wikimedia Commons)

During the Celtic festival of Samhain, when it was believed that souls from the Otherworld were able to cross over to the land of the living, the cult of the head reached a fever pitch. Armed with a plethora of root vegetables from the recent harvest (as Samhain marked the end of one pastoral year and the beginning of the next), ancient peoples carved frightening faces in an effort to ward off restless souls.

There was also a fire element to the festival of Samhain. On the night of October 31st, when the festival began, all fires burning across Ireland and other Celtic countries were supposed to be extinguished, and could only be rekindled thereafter from a ceremonial fire lit by druids. To facilitate this practice, a good deal of lanterns were needed to transport the coals. Hence, those carved root vegetables ended up serving a practical purpose in addition to a symbolic one. To quote Mannion:

"Metal lanterns were quite expensive, so people would hollow out root vegetables. Over time people started to carve faces and designs to allow light to shine through the holes without extinguishing the ember."

Of course, now we're faced with a chicken and the egg problem: Did the ancient Irish turn their carved faces into lanterns, as I suggested earlier, or did they carve faces into their lanterns, as Mannion asserts?

It's hard to say.

But what I can tell you definitively is that when the Christians arrived on the scene, they hijacked the festival of Samhain for their own purposes, turning November 1st into "All Saints' Day" a.k.a. "All Hallows." Hence, the evening prior became known as "All Hallows Eve," which is celebrated today as Halloween. The Celtic cult of the head was largely forgotten, and the vegetable lanterns with their frightening faces were reinterpreted, by some, as representations of Christian souls in purgatory.

The aforementioned Stingy Jack, of course, a man forever stuck between heaven and hell, fits that Christian interpretation to a T. So in addition to being used to explain the phenomenon of *ignis fatuus* and, later, to explain the origins of the jack-o'-lantern, the story of Jack was employed "as a cautionary tale, a morality tale," according to Mannion, who elaborates:

"Jack was a soul trapped between two worlds, and if you behaved like he did you could end up like that, too."

AMERICANIZATION OF THE JACK-O'-LANTERN: FROM TURNIPS TO PUMPKINS

If the history of the jack-o'-lantern wasn't already convoluted enough for ya, we have a whole 'nother era to explore — arguably the jack-o'-lantern's golden age:

The Age of Pumpkins.

In the midst of and in the decades following the Great Famine, millions of Irish immigrants fled to North America, and with them they brought their ancient Samhain/Halloween tradition of vegetable carving. While originally accustomed to using turnips, beets, and potatoes as their canvases, these Irish immigrants easily adapted their art to the more rotund and versatile pumpkin — a gourd native to the New World.

The first mention of the pumpkin jack-o'-lantern ostensibly appears in Nathaniel Hawthorne's 1835 short story, *The Great Carbuncle*, in which a band of adventurers seeks out a legendary gem. To quote Hawthorne:

"Hide it under thy cloak, say'st thou? Why, it will gleam through the holes, and make thee look like a jack-o'-lantern."

Given that *The Great Carbuncle* was written before the massive influx of Irish immigrants to North America, however, it is possible that Hawthorne is not actually referencing a pumpkin jack-o'-lantern in this passage, but the phenomenon of ignis fatuus. (Remember, that was the original meaning of the word.) That's not to say, however, that an earlier group of Irish immigrants couldn't have introduced the "carved vegetable lantern" meaning of jack-o'-lantern to Hawthorne. The matter is up for debate.

According to the *Irish Times*, the first definitive reference to a pumpkin jack-o'-lantern carved in celebration of Halloween occurred in 1886, when a Canadian newspaper, the *Daily News*, reported the following:

"The old time custom of keeping up Hallowe'en was not forgotten last night by the youngsters of the city [...]There was a great sacrifice of pumpkins from which to make transparent heads and face, lighted up by the unfailing two inches of tallow candle."

However, it should be noted that the first *image* of a pumpkin jack-o'-lantern appeared nearly two decades before this in the November 23, 1867 issue of *Harper's Weekly*. It was published alongside an article titled "A Pumpkin Effigy," but—and this is an important but—the article did not refer to the carved gourd as a "jack-o'-lantern," nor did it reference Halloween.

By the turn of the century, the pumpkin jack-o'-lantern had become the symbol of Halloween in North America. While once intended to scare off unwanted nocturnal visitors, these incandescent decorations are now most frequently used (despite their often grotesque appearances) to welcome visitors and convey a sense of joviality and community.

L.W. Atwater, "The Pumpkin Effigy," wood engraving, Harper's Weekly, Nov 23, 1867. Library of Congress, Washington, D.C., LC-USZ62-8391.

To quote Cindy Ott, author of *Pumpkin: The Curious History of an American Icon*:

"At Halloween, you don't go up to someone's house unless they have a jack-o'-lantern. It's about cementing a community, projecting good values, neighborliness. The pumpkin and jack-o'-lantern take on those meanings, too."

FINAL THOUGHT: THE NEVER-ENDING STORY

The jack-o'-lantern is an art form that has multiple possible origins (re: Celtic head veneration, an Irish folktale about an asshole, anonymous English night watchmen), multiple symbolic meanings (re: it represents the lantern of a notorious trickster, or the fires of Samhain, or Christian souls stuck in purgatory), and multiple functional purposes (re: transporting sacred coals, warding off evil spirits, welcoming guests). Which of these are the "correct" readings of the jack-o'-lantern's history? Perhaps none of them. Perhaps all of them. That's the beauty of a good story.

To quote Jessica Traynor, writing for the *Irish Times*:

"Stories rarely stay the same over time. They change, evolve, become symbol and metaphor – especially when people move to new places and different myths and cultures intermingle."

Here's to myths and cultures continuing to intermingle.

raises pumpkin sculpting tool

ABOUT THE AUTHOR

I. E. Kneverday is the mischief-maker-in-chief at IrishMyths.com, where he can be found plumbing the depths of Celtic mythology, Irish mythology, and Irish folklore. Go drop by and subscribe to stay up-to-date with his latest mythological musings.

Originally from the Boston area, Kneverday moved to Montréal at eighteen and promptly found employment in an Irish pub, first as a busboy and later as a folk musician. He left the pub occasionally to earn a degree in Humanistic Studies (minor: World Religions) from McGill University.

These days, Kneverday lives with his wife and two children (and two polydactyl cats) in San Jose, California. Does he miss the snow? Meh.

ALSO FROM
I. E. KNEVERDAY:

Irish Myths in Your Pocket
(Celtic Pocket Guides 1)

The perfect pocket-sized primer for
grasping the basics of Irish mythology,
including how it differs from Celtic
mythology; its main heroes, gods, and
monsters; and the many magical weapons
wielded on its battlefields.

Neon Druid: An Anthology of
Urban Celtic Fantasy

"A thrilling romp through pubs,
mythology, and alleyways. *NEON
DRUID* is such a fun, pulpy anthology of
stories that embody Celtic fantasy and
myth." —pylesofbooks.com

Printed in Poland
by Amazon Fulfillment
Poland Sp. z o.o., Wrocław

23408435R00097